Published by Clover Stornetta Farms
PO Box 750369
Petaluma, CA 94975

ISBN: 978-0-615-33536-0

Book Design: Anne Vernon as
VeVa Communications
51 E Street, Santa Rosa, CA 95404

Printed in 2010
Printed in Hong Kong through Global Interprint, Inc.
589 Mendocino Avenue
Santa Rosa, CA. 95401

I have had the great pleasure to work with Clover Stornetta Farms for fifteen years.
Clover never ceases to amaze me with its generosity, ethical code of conduct, and genuine concern for our community.
Oh, to have all companies follow their lead.

Thank you Joanie, you are wonderful and considerate to work with, and an asset to Clover beyond measure.
Thank you Margo, you have always been and continue to be a source of
steadfastness, support, and a great sounding board throughout the years of creativity.
And thanks to the public for your appreciation of our Clo.

Anne Vernon

Wholly Cow II

CLOVER STORNETTA FARMS
40 Years

A forty year historical retrospective of Clo the Cow's billboards

Text by Marcus Benedetti, Jim Benefield,
Gene Benedetti, and Anne Vernon
Executive Editor: Anne Vernon

Contributing Billboard Artists:
Anne Vernon, Gordon Cockroft, Art Zadina, Craig Curtiss, Susan Evason,
Bill Knight, Lynn Morgan, Bill Nellor, David Oshiro, and Jim Wakeman

Contributing Billboard Copywriters:
Jim Benefield, Anne Vernon, Margo VanMidde,
Dan Benedetti, Joanie Benedetti, and the much appreciated Public

After much popular demand, I have brought you the updated "Wholly Cow II."
Feast your eyes on a campaign that has graced California billboards for 40 years, always
punny, sometimes silly, often sweet, never jaded, and always worth a chuckle.
Yes, it is an advertising campaign, and all advertising campaigns are the
reflection of the company they represent. With that in mind, remember

I moo, therefore I am

My thanks to our late founder Gene Benedetti,
my beloved grandfather.

I also thank all our owners, Gary & Lynn Imm (retired), the late
John Markusen & his wife Pat, Kevin & Mary Imm (retired)
Herm & Marilyn Benedetti, Mike & Diane Keefer,
Mkulima & Diana Britt, my Mom & Dad, Anne & Dan Benedetti,
and of course my darling wife Mary Beth.

To all of our employees
& customers, you are all Clo's Friends.

Marcus Benedetti

Gene M. Benedetti, the founder of Clover Stornetta Farms, loving husband to Evelyn Benedetti, father of six, grandfather of 12 and great-grandfather of eleven has passed.

Although he is physically gone from us, he will never leave us. His legacy will live on.

It will live through Clo the Cow, Clover's mascot whom Gene created, the partners of Clover and the family of employees.

It will live through Gene and Evelyn's six children, two of whom are following in his footsteps at Clover.

It will live through Gene and Evelyn's 12 grandchildren, four of whom are following in his footsteps at Clover.

It will live through his love for community and generosity to give to those less fortunate.

It will live through his heroic efforts in WWII and the invasion of Normandy on D day.

For those who were fortunate to know Gene know that this larger than life man will always be with us.

Interview with Gene Benedetti

Founder and patriarch for Clover Stornetta Farms
Interviewed by Anne Vernon

Back around 1951 Lee Levinger came to me in Petaluma and said, "I want to do some advertising for you." He knew that Clover was new in Santa Rosa, and I knew we needed help.

Lee was Clover's first ad man. I had a lot of respect for him because his mind was always going. He became quite a person in Santa Rosa, and in Sonoma County.

He eventually came up with this idea that we should have a billboard. I said, "Lee, you're crazy. Marin County just voted to eliminate billboards. I don't want to make enemies with anybody. Billboards aren't going to be well liked."

Lee said, "I want to do something totally different on a billboard. It will be a series. I want to have a play on words that's going to be very interesting and people are going to anticipate them, and they're going to enjoy them. There will be no hard sell. It will be about happiness, and the good things about Clover. I'm going to develop a cow or something that's a caricature."

So about two-three weeks later he gave me a call. We'd always go to lunch

The original Clo-the-Cow was first drawn in a sixties-style line drawing by Bill Nellor, the art director for Lee Levinger. He revised it to the current smiling Clo a year later.

and have a couple martinis, and we'd sit there and shake dice and have a lot of fun, but we'd also conduct business. He had this board, done in freehand himself! And he said, "Now look, this is not the final version of what I want, but I did this, and I'm not an artist. And you can tell as soon as I show it to you that I'm not an artist, but I didn't want to get an artist involved until I could get some kind of approval from you to go ahead with this."

I looked at it and here was a facsimile of Clo—not really the Clo that we have or that we had then even. This was Clo out in a field, and on the top it said "Outstanding in her Field." I liked the idea.

I took it to the Board, put it on the agenda, and I explained what we were doing. One of the board members leaned aside and looked at his secretary. He was an outspoken character and got up and said, "Dammit, Gene, if we're going to have a billboard,—first of all, people don't want billboards now—but if we're going to have a billboard I want a real cow on it!"

I said, "I appreciate your feelings, but we think this is something that will really generate interest." They all sat up, and another one got up and said, "We agree wholeheartedly, we want a real cow."

I said, "You're missing the whole point." But after going round and round, it was finally passed! And the rest is history.

Interview with Marcus Benedetti

President of Clover Stornetta Farms
Interviewed by Anne Vernon

As part of the third generation of the Clover family, I was brought up by my Pops, Gene Benedetti and my Dad, Dan Bendetti, to value how people, our environment, and our farms were treated. We valued sustainability before there was ever a word for it.

Clover was always one of the smallest independent dairies in the state of California, and as such we had to do things very differently than the rest of our peers in the industry. With pharmaceutical companies introducing new ways of dairying, Clover took a step back and evaluated what was right for our producers and consumers. Since Clover was the first to adamantly market the fact that we don't use hormones in our product, that set us apart and put us on a path towards what we call today our North Coast Excellence Certified Program.

The four tenets we formulated for the program were our philosophy of life, really. First, 100% of our milk comes from cows not treated with rBST. Instead of relying on rBST for increased milk production, Clover recognized that reducing animal stress, managing our cows in small herds, and closely monitoring the health of our animals was more sustainable, more ethical, and more profitable for us, our farmers, and our consumers.

Second was preservation of the family dairy farms on the North Coast. Our farmers are our families, and some of our farmers are fourth generation family operations. Theses legacies are invaluable, because they embody the best of environmental stewardship, and the American values of love for our beautiful country, our families, and a time honored way of life.

The third was Sustainable Agriculture, which went right along with our family farms' way of life. We also had been paying attention to what our consumers were caring about, and demanding in dairy products. We realized quite quickly that they cared about how the land is being treated that produced the product. As a result, we embarked on a sustainability program with all our family farms that contained a concrete program with third party certification.

Finally, quality milk products are what we produce, with all the care and concern for the systems we have instituted to produce it. The next time you're shopping for milk ask yourself the question; has my dairy addressed the issues that are important to me and family? Like, where does my milk come from? How clean is it? How are the dairy families being compensated? We at Clover have addressed these issues and always will. That's our commitment to you and your family.

Marcus Benedetti, President of Clover Stornetta Farms, with the Stornettas at their farm at Point Arena.

Nourishing and Maintaining Our Family Farms

Clover has been at the forefront of the movement to buy locally and invest in our family farms. To ensure this, Clover Stornetta Farms instituted a program called "North Coast Excellence Certified" (NCEC) in 1994, which guarantees all Clover milk is from Marin, Sonoma, and Mendocino counties only, and that our cows are not treated with the growth hormone rBST.

Clover's sustainable agricultural practices and the ultra high standards of our NCEC program ensure the future of our family farms here on the North Coast. Our select group of small family farms, as a pool, produce the highest quality milk in the United States—quality based on coliform counts, standard plate counts, and somatic cell counts. Clover rewards these families for their use of these progressive farm practices. Clover's methods of sustainable agriculture are founded on the premise of being economically viable, environmentally sound and socially responsible.

The clean roadside appearance of our ranches reflects the superior milk products within. Ranchers must maintain 90 percent ranch scores, and ongoing dairy upgrades. Dairies awarded the NCEC certification do not use rBST, the genetically engineered bovine growth hormone that stimulates milk production. Milk from cows not treated with rBST alleviates concern about potential human health risks from the synthetic hormone. To date, this hormone has been banned in milk production in Europe, Canada, and at Clover, but not in the United States. We know where 100 percent of our milk comes from and guarantee that it is 100 percent rBST free.

- *Clover produces some of the cleanest milk products in the United States, rated far above state and federal standards.*

- *Clover Dairy's average milking herd is approximately 300 cows, and average ranch sizes are over 500 acres. This is a smaller than average herd size with ample pasture land.*

- *The bucolic fields along the North Coast of California provide an ideal climate and pasture for Clover cows.*

Our Family of Farms

Robert Giacomini Dairy

Bivalve Dairy

JLT Ranch

Lafranchi Dairy

Triple C Ranch

Al Stornetta, Gene Benedetti & Charlie Stornetta,
Clover Stornetta Farms, circa 1977.

Al & Charlie were the first Clover Stornetta Family Farm.

Walter Stornetta Ranch
& Del Mar Farms

Perucchi Dairy

Bodega Farms

McClelland Dairy

Rancho Laguna Dairy

DeBernardi Family Dairy

McCall Dairy

Moretti Family Dairy

Kehoe Dairy

Amos Brothers

Gillian's Dairy

Bucher Farms

Jim Riebli Dairy

*Bordessa Dairy &
Ocean Breeze Dairy*

McClure Dairy

Robert & Jolynn McClelland Dairy

Neil McIsaac & Son Dairy

Sustainable in Thought, Word & Deed

Sustainable Agriculture is more than just a "buzz" word. Clover uses economic viability, environmental stewardship, and social responsibility as our definition of sustainable agriculture. That definition guides us through our daily business practices.

Consumers want to know where their milk comes from. We source our milk every day from family farms on the North Coast of California. It is important to Clover that these families remain a viable and integral part of our community. The same family farms deliver their milk to Clover every day of the year and twelve of the dairies are certified organic. All of Clover's dairies operate closed herds, breeding and raising their own calves, and not purchasing them on the open market helps to protect the bio-security of the farms. Clover's story is unique to the industry.

Also very important to Clover is our dedication to animal welfare. It is an increasing concern amongst consumers. In September 2000, Clover Stornetta Farms was the first dairy in the United States to be awarded the American Humane Certified label for humanely produced dairy products.

With this certification, our cows are free from hunger and thirst because of ready access to water and a healthful diet. They are free from discomfort because of ample shelter and living space. They are free to share the company of their own kind, and they are free from unnecessary pain, injury, and disease.

In 1994, Clover Stornetta became the first dairy processor to elevate milk from a commodity to a specialty food by establishing the NCEC program. NCEC purity standards are the strictest in the dairy industry, far surpassing the state and federal governments'. Clover tests the raw milk delivered to its plant daily to protect against antibiotic residues. The milk is also tested for bacteria, coliform and somatic cell count, to ensure Clover's customers are getting the cleanest glass of milk possible. Clover's North Coast Excellence Ceritfied Program has an independent auditor that verifies Clover's milk quality standards, represented by the North Coast Excellence Certified Seal on its carton.

Clover Stornetta Farms was honored in 2003 when Sustainable Northwest, based in Portland, Oregon, named Clover as one of the recipients of the Founders of a New Northwest award. Sustainable Northwest was established in 1997 with recognition that human communities and natural systems in the Pacific Northwest were suffering under the existing economic development

model. The award recognizes the innovative work Clover has done to build a sustainable economy in the Northwest, and reads: "For refusing to sacrifice the good of the land for the good of the people or the good of the people for the good of the land-finding a new path which honors both. For giving of yourself to a vision of the human community working together-able to think beyond itself to embrace the entire biological community and from one generation to many."

Clover Stornetta Farms was one of the first dairies in the United States to receive the HACCP certification. The HACCP system, which stands for Hazard Analysis of Critical Control Points, was conceived as a systemic and systematic program to ensure food safety. Its principles were developed in the 1960's for application in the NASA space foods program but recently, it has gained acceptance as the fundamental food safety system throughout the world. HACCP was conceived as a series of steps which are integrated into a coherent, systematic and relatively simple system whose main purpose is to minimize the probability of unacceptable hazard impact; this translates into risk control at all points of the food chain.

On behalf of Sustainable Business Institute, Congresswoman Lynn Woolsey presented Clover Stornetta Farms the Seal of Sustainability™ in Washington D.C. at a Congressional briefing on October 23, 2007. Clover Stornetta is one of seven companies in the world to be recognized with the Seal of Sustainability™. The seal recognizes Clover as being a business leader in the acceptance and adaptation of sustainable economic, social, and environmental business practices.

"I want to congratulate everyone at Clover for winning this important award. But I'm not surprised that Clover Stornetta is being recognized for its socially responsible policies," said Congresswoman Lynn Woolsey. "Gene, who was a founder of the company, was well known for his commitment to the community. They like to say, 'Enjoy Clover Products in Good Conscience and in Good Health,' that's not just a slogan, it's a real promise to Clover Stornetta's customers — a promise Clover Stornetta keeps everyday."

Over the years Clover has worked hard to be a more sustainable company. In addition to the work it has done with the family farms that deliver milk to Clover, some of the achievements Clover has made include; developing a local source of organic milk to decrease its miles to market; converting its fleet to cold plate technology which charges Clover's trucks at night using substantially less energy than cooling all day long with diesel; installing a 32 kilowatt solar system in its fleet maintenance facility; installing a new waste water system that reduces Clover's water consumption by 10 million gallons a year; and the list goes on.

Clover Stornetta Farms is a three generation family owned and operated dairy processor in California.
Tip Clo through your two lips and taste the difference!

Sustainable farming is family farming; an ideal at its best.

Community & Giving

Clover's philosophy has structured our company and the quality of our dairy products. We have chosen to place extraordinary quality of product and quality of life first. Taking care of community is equally important. Clover has an on line store where people can purchase merchandise, and the proceeds from "Clo's Line" of merchandise go to the Clover Stornetta Fund at the Community Foundation of Sonoma County. These funds are used on projects sustaining social, environmental and agricultural endeavors. For the past eight years Clover has sponsored Clo's Classic, a football game with the SRJC Bear Cubs. Proceeds from this annual event go to charities the Bear Cub players choose.

Here are just some of the causes Clover has contributed to over the years:

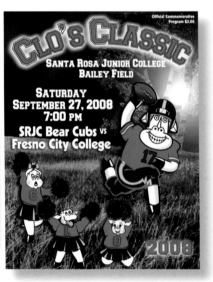

Thank You to Clo's Family

Clover's Amazing Staff

Andrew Adams
Steven Adams
Richard Albertoni
Mariano Arriaza
Christopher Bacher
Michael Baker
Joseph Balistreri
Jon Barnes
David Barry
Herm Benedetti
Dante Benedetti
Marcus Benedetti
Joanie Benedetti
Michael Benedetti
Donald Blair
Matt Bloom
Kevin Brant
Kristian Bredahl
Mkulima Britt
Bob Brown
Keith Brumbley
Mark Bunting
Shawn Burnside
Daniel Butler
Ed Byrne
Alan Casey
Paul Cass
Ross Christensen
James Clark
Robert Cotta
Larry Crozier
Cynthia Cruise

Stacy Davis
Brian Davis
Andrew Del Carlo
Julie Del Curto
Hoai-Phuong Doan
Carlene Dolcini
Paul Drake
William Drake
Michael Drew Sr
Kathy Duncan
Karen Dunigan
Michael Dusek
Thomas Edwards
David Elliott
Douglas Erlendson
Gustavo Escobar
Lisa Estes
Brad Evart
Michael Fisicaro
Adrian Flores
William Garlinghouse
Dayna Ghirardelli
Leela Godino
Kenneth Gomes
Carlos Gonzalez
Janna Gossner
Michael Griffin
Julie Gullickson
Andrew Haaf
William Hagle
Kifle Haile
Harry Hall

Ronald Halvorson
Michael Hamilton
Harlan Hansen
Adam Hansen
Devin Harrington
Don Heid
Gene Heinlein
Donald Hendrickson
George Henning
Manuel Hernandez

Daniel Hernandez
Clifford Hollenbeck
Stacy Hopkins
Matthew Huber
Pete Hulsman
Florin Iancu
Gary Imm
Kevin Imm
Michael Jacobsen
Judy James

Philip Jensen
Jeffrey Jones
Tina Kane
Andrew Keefer
Michael Keefer
Kenny Kehoe
Brian Kemp
Thomas King
Dennis King
Christopher Kirby

Andrew Krieg
James Krist
William Kruljac Jr
Richard Kruml
Kenneth Kuhn
Edward Kvidahl
Rodney Lacy Sr.
Philippe Landier
Jimmy Lane
Joanne Leveroni-Wood

Kevin Lewis
William Lewis
Nicholas Linale
Judith Linale
Peter Linale
Andrea Lohner
Martin Lorenzo
Samuel Lozano
Erik Lozano
Jose Lozano

Lorena Lozano
Sean Lukas
Timothy Manning
Ronald Markovich
Ronald Markovich II
Paul Masuero
Michael Matteri
Michael McCarthy
Matthew McConnell
Marcia McGlochlin

Michael McIntosh
Nohl McKenna
Gail McLaughlin
Jeffery McMellon
Ora McMellon
Jorge Mejia
Randy Menke
Thomas Merriott
James Miller
Izzy Mojica

Ozzie Mojica
Jose Luis Mojica
Alfredo Monter
Robert Morgan
Brian Mount
Donald Murray
William Names
Fredrick Naredo
Gino Norris
Keith Norris

Elliott Olivarez
Robert Olsen
Anita Ortega
Lance Papka
Todd Parks
Darrell Peloquin
Scott Pelton
Randy Pierce
Earnest Pigg
Joseph Policarpo
Craig Pomeroy
Ronald Pomeroy
Thomas Powers
Sylvia Proctor
John Quinliven
Ricardo Ramos Rico
Nicholas Ramponi
Brian Redding
Jason Reed
Christopher Ricci
Ted Roberts
David Robinson

Mike Robinson
Emiterio Rojas
Rick Rosario
John Ruzsicska
Felix Sanchez-Monter
Naomi Schmitt
Chris Scott
Elizabeth Selya
Andrew Shaw
Manuel Silva

Joseph Silva
Craig Simi
Dean Singleton
Jack Skilling
Louis Smith
Timothy Snowden
Jerry Sprague
Robert St Clair
Michael Staricka
Randy Stewart
Mark Strika
Muhammad Tariq
Virgil Thompson
Maurice Thompson
Jorge Torres
Kevin Vaughn
Ramon Velarde
David Visser
Karen Vollbrecht
Mark Walker
Ronald Wesner
Tony Weston
Richard White
Ryan White
Scott Williams
David Willis
Howard Woldemar
Thomas Woodville
Michael Zaccagna
Edward Zentner
Arthur Zimmer

The Beginning:

Interview with Jim Benefield, former Chairman of Benefield, Levinger, McEndy & Vernon, who retired in 1995 after 41 years in journalism, public relations and advertising.

For 20 years I carried on a love affair with a chubby-cheeked cutie with pointed ears and big teeth. Her name is Clo, the affable bovine who is everyone's favorite cow. Clo sprang from the pen of Bill Nellor, an art director for Lee Levinger's Santa Rosa ad agency, in 1968. This early rendition looked more like a real cow than the one we know and love today. She wasn't particularly appealing, so in 1969 Bill revised her into a cartoon character that has survived with minor changes for over 40 years. Bill left the agency in 1970, replaced by Chris Alderman at the drawing board.

I bought the ad agency from Lee in 1972, although Lee stayed on to work with Clover for several more years. With Mike Fitzpatrick now doing the artwork, boards such as "Clearly ahead," featuring an inflated likeness of Clo's head bursting through the panel, appeared on Highway 101. For two decades I abandoned conscience to come up with the most outrageous puns I could devise or steal, starting with "Clo's line."

Through the years an outstanding succession of artists have worked on the Clo billboards, including Jim Wakeman, Bill Knight, Craig Curtiss, Susan Evason, David Oshiro, Lynn Morgan, Gordon Cockroft, Anne Vernon, and Art Zadina.

Gene Benedetti & Jim Benefield in front of the 1981 inflated version of "Clearly Ahead."

I would like to pontificate about the studies, surveys, blind tastings, copy testing and focus group interviews that contributed to developing a complex marketing strategy for Clover. Unfortunately, because ad men are noted for their humility and candor, I can't. The Clover campaign is based on a couple of obvious points: the client produces an excellent product, and the advertising for something as basic as milk should be kept simple.

Clover advertising in the '50's and early '60's concentrated on building a local image for the dairy — "Aren't you glad you live in Clover Country," featuring scenes of happy young families enjoying Clover Milk in such settings as the redwoods or aboard a Russian River canoe. With the advent of Clo in 1969 this theme became "Support your local cow" and "Local girl makes good," highlighted by the broadly smiling cartoon cow.

Clo was created as a mascot to represent the company, to project a warm, friendly, down home feeling for the dairy and to generate loyalty for its products. That she has succeeded over the last four decades is indicated by the fact that early on she wore a bell around her neck labeled "Clo," so people would know who she was. It would be difficult to find a person in the area today who couldn't identify her. She was chosen one year to be Grand Marshal of Santa Rosa's Rose Parade, and in 1995, the Sonoma County Museum put on a special exhibition tracing her career.

After the "local" boards came a series in a lighter vein, such as "The Producer," with Clo attired as a Hollywood mogul, complete with dark glasses; "Factory Fresh," with Clo sporting a smokestack; and "The Now Cow," with

Clo decked out in psychedelic colors.

The infamous puns came next, starting with "Outstanding in her field" and "Clearly ahead." Two of the favorites came from a 1989 contest for billboard ideas—announced in a message on a milk carton—that attracted 7,481 entries. Top winner, with "Tip Clo through your two lips," was Ally Minatta of Sonoma. Second price, for "Splendor in the glass," went to Helen Vanderbilt of San Anselmo.

Clo has not been limited to billboards. She shows up in newspaper and magazine ads, school yearbooks and football programs, radio commercials, and an award-winning series of television spots that combined live action with animation to bring three of the billboards to life. A dozen years ago the ad agency embarked on a major redesign project that now features Clo on the packaging for the full line of Clover Stornetta products. And the agency designed an eight-foot, inflatable, walk-around figure of Clo, which appears in parades, store openings and civic events of all kinds. In addition to their roadside locations, the billboards get wide circulation by being painted on the sides of Clover's fleet of trucks.

Through the years the Clover billboards have won a wide array of advertising industry awards, local, national and international. The most prestigious recognition came in 1991 when the agency won the top award in the billboard campaign category of the International Advertising Festival of New York, which attracted 3,790 entries from 40 countries. The three boards submitted were "Supreme Quart," with Clo in judicial robes; "Half Galleon," with Clo at sea in pirate garb; and "Splendor in the Glass," with Clo in a flower-filled meadow. Runners-up to the Clover entry were campaigns for Volkswagen, produced by DDB Needham Worldwide of Detroit, and British Aerospace, produced by Austin Knight Advertising Limited of London.

How long can this lighthearted ad campaign go on? As long as Clo continues to bring smiles to the faces of her fans, young and old, and as long as they continue to enjoy the milk lovingly produced by this amiable bovine. There are still plenty of delicious puns in the barrel, eager to burst forth for the amusement of Clo's friends.

These three boards were top winners in the billboard campaign

category of the 1991 International Advertising Festival of New York.

Thoughts About Clo as a Cartoon Cow

...or remembering to remember **CLO *IS* A CARTOON COW!**

Working with a cow named Clo is a gift. It makes you think in terms of gentleness and chuckles. Sometimes while sipping my glass of Clover milk and working on a billboard idea, I think of Caspar the Ghost, or my dog Butchie. These are two other softly good-natured creatures that remind me of Clo. Whenever I'm in doubt about a turn of Clo's leg, or a three quarter view of Clo's shoulder, I often use my dog, short, stocky and plump-legged, as my artist model for Clo. And Caspar and Clo could be in the same cartoon and look like they were family!

One thing about working with Clo over a very long period of time is that she doesn't age like humans do. After all, she is a cartoon cow. We decided to plump her up about fourteen years ago, not because she was getting older, but because we wanted her body to look less...human! (And somewhat more androgenous. That really helps when you are switching back and forth between the male and female outfits). Another great thing about Clo...even when she's undressed, she still looks dressed!

Just putting Clo in an ad is a thing of beauty. It's like working with a fairy tale. Or Dairy Tail! And with any long running campaign, it's important to evolve and improve without changing the essence of the message. Therefore, we introduced the Clo Babies in the 2002 billboard "Dairy Tails." It expanded the cartoon narrative story lines tremendously.

We hope that you continue to enjoy Clo in her wonderful world, because she genuinely reflects the company she is the spokescow for. It works like this. In order to have a lasting advertising campaign that is genuine and effective, you must have an excellent product. The marketing message must transparently show what the company stands for, and clearly reflect its values. Clo does just that. She is the vision and philosophy of Clover Stornetta Farms, with their care for their community, their environment, and their steady, complete dedication to producing the best dairy products in the world. After all, Clo's products are made with the "Milk of Human Kindness"!

Anne Vernon, Creative Director

CLOVER STORNETTA FARMS

40 Years

1969-2009 A Retrospective: 40 years of Clo's Billboards

support your local cow...

buy Clover milk

Pilgrims brought cows to America. The first cow in America arrived in the Jamestown colony in 1611.

1969

CLOVER
the only milk with LOVE in it.

A cow's heart weighs about 5lbs and pumps
400 pints of blood through the udder to produce 1 pint of milk.
That means nearly 10,000 pints of blood are pumped
through a cow's udder daily to produce 3 gallons of milk.

THE NOW COW

hours fresher Clover Milk

"THE NOW COW" billboard featured Clo with a hippie headband, attired in the psychedelic colors of the '70s.
"The Now Cow," always with it, produced her milk right now, guaranteeing that fresh Clover taste.
 The Now Cow was redone in 2001 and is featured on page 109.

1970

FOR GOODNESS SAKE
Drink Clover Milk

A Holstein's spots are like fingerprints.
No two cows have the same spots.

MOOVE UP TO CLOVER MILK

Q: How do you know that cows will be in Heaven?

A: It's a place of udder delight!

Also ran as "It's Great to Live in Clover Country," 1972

Clover Milk
GIVE IT A WHIRL

Loclomotion

Nearly every family had its own cow until the 1850's. The first regular shipment of milk by railroad was between Orange County, New York, and New York City and began in 1841.

1971

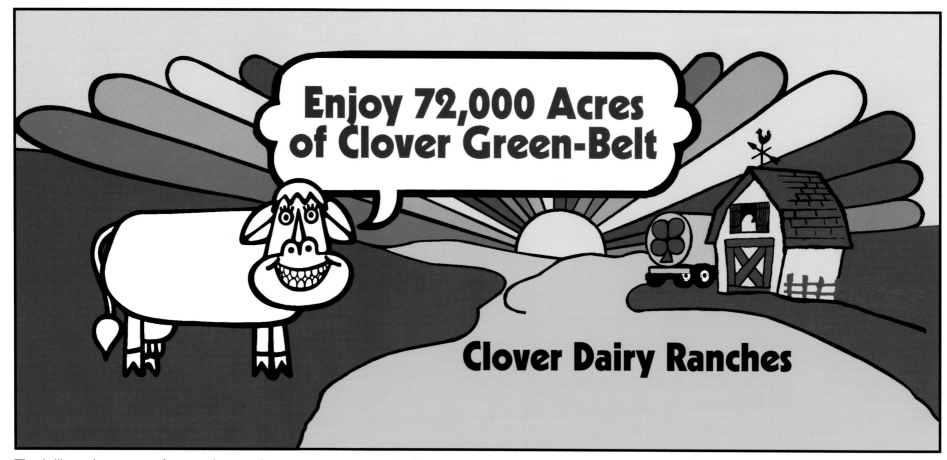

This billboard was part of an outdoor and newspaper campaign highlighting the contribution Clover dairy ranches made to preserving the green hills and rural atmosphere of Clover Country. Clover Stornetta Farms remains committed to sustainable agriculture to this day.

1974

"Clo's line" was the first of the long run of pun-driven billboards, each more outrageous than the last.

"Outstanding in her field" showed a bell around Clo's neck with her name on it, to help establish name recognition for the lovable bovine early in her career.

My cup runneth Clover

Dairy cows provide 90% of the world's milk supply.
Water buffalo, camels, goats, sheep, horses,
and reindeer are also milked.

1979

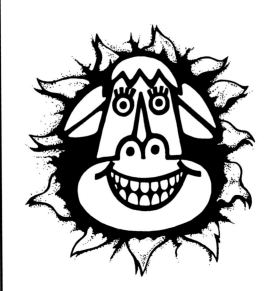

Clearly Ahead

"Clearly Ahead" featured an inflated version of Clo's head bursting through the billboard. Shown here are Gene Benedetti and Jim Benefield in front of the Highway 101 board.

During the billboard's run, the 3-D inflatable cow head was removed from the billboard in the middle of the night. The mystery remains as to who took it!

Mooin' pitcher star

Why does a milking stool have only three legs?

A: Because the cow has the udder!

Clo's uncounters
of the curd kind

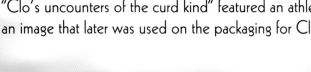

"Clo's uncounters of the curd kind" featured an athletic running Clo, an image that later was used on the packaging for Clover's low-fat products.

Cows have 32 teeth:
- 8 incisors on the bottom front...
- 6 molars on the top and bottom of each side...
- A tough pad of skin instead of teeth on the top front!

1984

Q: What do you use to feed a dinosaur milk?

A: A dinosaucer!

Supreme Quart

This board was one of three boards (including **Splendor in the Glass** and **Half Galleon**), that won in the prestigious International Advertising Festival of New York for top billboard campaign.

The headline for "Supreme Quart" came from Jim Miller, driver of one of Clover's 40-foot tractor-trailers.

1985

The average body temperature of a cow is 101.5°F. Cows can see color. Cows have almost total 360-degree panoramic vision.

Q: Why should you never-ever tell a cow a secret?

A: Because it will go in one ear and out the udder!

1986

Clo's look

"Clo's look" and "New designer Clos" were part of the campaign to introduce a new package design for Clover products, for the first time, including illustrations of Clo.

New designer Clos

Q: What do you get if you cross a cow with a spaniel, a poodle, and a rooster?

This illustration was done to help the Sonoma County Humane Society.

A: A cockerpoodlemoo!

1986

My Fair Lady
Sonoma
County Fair

July 27 - August 9
Santa Rosa

"My Fair Lady" helped promote the Sonoma County Fair, and called attention to one of the Fair's prime attractions, the Clover ice cream booth, where patrons could beat the heat with free ice cream cones. In 2009 alone, Clover gave out over 75,000 ice cream cones for both the Sonoma County and Sonoma Marin Fairs!

1987

Always ready to promote culture, Clo offered some of the great composer's piano music on this board.
The music could actually be heard as part of a TV commercial that combined animation and live action,
bringing the billboard to life.

1987

The Clover brand name celebrated its 75th Anniversary!

Clo's horse

Sonoma County Fair
Fairgrounds • Santa Rosa • July 20-Aug.4

The average cow weighs about 1,400 pounds!

1988

Half Galleon

Clo rides the high seas on one of three billboards brought to life, combining animation and live action, for a TV commercial.
The skill of animator Damon Rarey showed Clo firing her cannon across the bow of Gene and Dan Benedetti's passing convertible.

This board was also one of three boards (including **Supreme Quart** and **Splendor in the Glass**), that won in the International Advertising Festival of New York for top billboard campaign.

1988

The gestation for a cow is nine months, with the average newborn weight 80 to 100 pounds. Cows can live up to 25 years.

1988

Christopher Cowlumbus in the Moo World

Your body needs calcium for strong bones and teeth. The best way to get calcium is from milk and other milk group foods. To get enough calcium you need at least three servings of dairy products a day!

Miss Sonoma Cownty

1988

Q: Why did the blonde buy a brown cow?

A: To get chocolate milk!

van Clo's favorite pitcher

Note van Clo's left ear. The original painting by van Clo still exists.

Q: In what other billboards is Clo a painter?

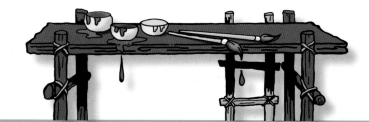

A: Michelangelo (2001), and Claude Moonet (1993).

Mooin' over the dessert

For the Gourmet
CLO'S CHOICE
Ice Cream

1989

Tip Clo through your two lips

The headline for this board won the top prize in a 1989 contest that drew 7,481 billboard ideas. Ally Minatta of Sonoma was the winner.

Second prize in the 1989 contest went to Helen Vanderbilt of San Anselmo for this headline.

This board was also one of three boards (including **Supreme Quart** and **Half Galleon**), that won in the International Advertising Festival of New York for top billboard campaign.

1989

Two Clos' fur comfort.

Q: In what other billboards are there lions, and tigers, and bears?
(Oh My!)

A: The Greatest Clo on Earth (1993),
Clo's up & purrsonal (1997),
& Clodilocks (1999)!

This board was also brought to life as a TV commercial, featuring Clo on a foggy runway in Casablanca, ready to share some Clover Ice Cream.

Light up your life!

NEW from CLOVER

CLOVER
STORNETTA
LOWFAT Milk 1%

CLOVER
STORNETTA
1% LOWFAT Milk
HALF GALLON (1.89 Liters)

Q: What is the name of Clo's space craft?

A: U.F. Clo

Moona Lisa

A classic pitcher.

A perfect classic.

Cowabunga!

The famed poster by Toulouse-Lautrec provided the multi-talented Clo with an opportunity to demonstrate her skill as a high-kicking cancan dancer.

1991

Moooy bueno

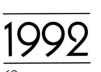

1992
62

Here's how to say Moo in 16 different languages...
Australia- Maaaate • Chile- Mmmuo • Finland- Ammuu! • France- Mooí
Germany- Mü • Guam- Moohaki • Israel- "mem" followed by "vav"
Japan- Mu-san • Latin- Mugio (I moo) • Netherlands- Boe (pronounced "Boo")
New Zealand- Moou • Norway- Møe • Poland- Mööski
Québec- Meuh! • Spain- Muu • Sweden- Muuuuuh!

It's not Clover 'til the fat lady sings!

Again demonstrating Clo's dedication to the arts, everyone's favorite cow performs in grand opera as the star soprano, probably in an opus by Wagner.

1992

Clo's Friends

Q: Which billboards have Clo with boats?

A: Half Galleon (1988),
Christopher Cowlumbus in the Moo World (1988),
Mooby Dick (1996),
and White Sips of Clover (2000)

The Greatest Clo on Earth

Q: Which billboards show Clo as a Queen?

A: Her Moojesty (1994), Anthony & Cleopatra (1995),
Miss Sonoma County (1988)

The gardens of Giverny could be anywhere.

Going Green: Clover was a forerunner of recycling, done in conjunction with a national recycling effort. **Solar Power:** In June 2008, Clover Stornetta completed the "Fleet Maintenance Facility Solar Project". Nearly 100% of the entire building's energy needs are now supplied by our 32 kilowatt solar system. This is the equivalent of eliminating over 61,000 pounds of CO_2 annually. **Cold Plate Technology:** Clover uses cold plate technology (instead of diesel fuel) in our refrigerated trucks. Charging the trucks at night uses substantially less energy than cooling all day long with diesel. Annual CO_2 emissions are reduced by over 236,000 lbs as a result. This technology is cleaner, quieter, and better for the planet.

1993

Clo commemorates the 50th Anniversary of "D" Day.

Her Moojesty

Clo was the reigning queen of hearts at the Renaissance Faire at Black Point, in Novato, California.

Q: What's a cow barn on a holiday?

A: A Merry Dairy!

1994

Venus de Moolo

CLOVER
STORNETTA
Vitamin D
Milk

CLOVER
STORNETTA

Vitamin D
Milk

HALF GALLON (1.89 Liters)

Q: In how many billboards does Clo appear as a male*?
As a female*? As just Clo?

*(In order to qualify as male or female, it must be an outfit that only one gender traditionally wears, not one that both can wear.

A: Male: 33
Female: 33
As Clo: 78

Clo's encownter

Marine World Africa USA
13 miles

Clo's next encownter with Marine World.

Q: In how many billboards does Clo appear with a marine animal?

A: Six.
Cowabunga (1990),
Clo's Friends (1993),
Clo's encownter (Above),
Mooby Dick (1996),
Eclological (1999),
and Moomaids (2001)

1994

Moovin' right along...

CLOVER
STORNETTA FARMS

Udderly Silly:

Q: What do you call a cow that plays the guitar?

A: A moosician!

At Clo's range

Q: Which billboard has camels?

A: Mooin over the dessert (1987)

Clo shows up as the umpire at a Crushers game, a local professional baseball team, where she calls the team's mascot, the Abominable Sonoman, safe at home.

Clo's theory of extraordinary milk.

Center Quart

Q: How many different sports does Clo play (in the billboards only)?

1995

A: Seventeen!!!
Rope Twirling (Clover Milk Give it a Whirl, 1971)
Track & Field (Clo's uncounters of the curd kind, 1982)
Hot Air Balloon Racing (Light up your life, 1990)
Surfing (Cowabunga, 1990)
Scuba Diving (Clo's Friends, 1993)
Roller Skating (Moovin' right along..., 1994)
Baseball (Clo's Call, 1995 ● Pitcher Perfect, 2007)
Tennis (Center Quart, 1995)

Anthony & Clopatra

Continued from page 76

Football (Scooper Bowl, 1995 • Clover Achiever 2007)
Aerial Acrobatics (Clo's hangar, 1996)
Anything Olympian? (Clo for the Gold, 1996)
Motor Car Racing (Clo's Race: 1999, • Mooovin' at Sears Point, 2000
NASCOW, 2001, • Pour It On, 2002)

Boating (The White Sips of Clover, 2000)
Bowling (Udderly Striking, 2000)
Motocycle Racing (Litre of the Pack, 2003)
Horseback Riding (Camoolot, 2004 • Lady Clodiva, 2005)
Skygliding (Mooin' in the Wind, 2007)
Wrestling (Sumoo Wrestling, 2008)

Scooper Bowl

Inducted into the Pro Football Hall of Fame in 1990, Bob St. Clair enjoys working with Clo in the San Francisco area, his old stomping ground with the 49ers.

In 2001, as a tribute for playing a total of 17 seasons and 189 home games at Kezar Stadium, the city of San Francisco renamed the stadium's field in honor of St. Clair.

Clo's hangar

Clo is a daredevil flyer in this adventure scene.

Mooby Dick

CLOVER STORNETTA FARMS

Cow Facts:

Cows drink about a bathtub full of water and eat around 40 pounds of food a day!

Clo's vintage herds appeared in both Napa and Sonoma counties.

Dairy Godmother

Fact: Clo has appeared as a fairy in Dairy Godmother, and as an angel when she is the spokescow for Clover's low milk bacteria counts. She loves to wear wings and fly (among other things)!

1996

	Bacteria Count	Coliform	Somatic Cell Count
US	300,000	No regs	750,000
California	50,000	750	600,000
Clover's Average*	1,803	47	168,209

* Lab tests averages for 2008

This board is the one and only without our Clo.

1996

Cloverland Express

Q: Which billboard has a dinosaur?

A: Clo Magnum (1985)

Clo won her very own gold during the 1996 Summer Olympics.

Clo's inspection

Clover Stornetta Farms had embarked upon a public relations move to promote their North Coast Excellence Certified Program, which proclaimed their philosophy of extraordinarily high standards for their milk. This included bacteria and coliform counts far lower than state and federal standards, and the decision not to include the bovine growth hormone (rBST), now banned in Canada, Europe, and Clover, but allowed in the United States.

CLOreogHEIFER

Clo trimmed some 150 pounds off her buxom frame during her short-lived but satisfying career as a dancer and personal trainer.

1996

Quart Jester

Q: Why did the cow wear a bell around her neck?

A: Because her horn didn't work!

Clo White and the seven Quarts

"Clo White" is a favorite of Clo's fans. During its development process, it had a record-breaking amount of toadstool revisions.

A cow can detect odors
up to five miles away.

1997

Clo's up and purrrsonal

Clo and Marine World (before it was Six Flags), promote healthy food and entertainment together.

Q: What's a cow's favorite moosical key?

A: Beef flat.

Mt. Rushmoooer

Q: What does a cow like to do by a campfire?

A: Roast mooshmallows!

As in all the billboards, the agency researched history to make sure "Cowpernicus" was appropriately attired, and with the correct instruments. Though originally we thought Cowpernicus would have a telescope, we discovered that at that time, they had not been invented. Instead, Cowpernicus was equipped with an historically correct sextant.

1997

Clover Coaster

Clover again joined up with Six Flags New Marine World Theme Park, with the artist's rendition of a special rollercoaster created in her name!

Q: What do cows like to do at amoosement parks?

Edgar Allan Clo

This is considered a quintessential Clo billboard: simple, direct, with elegance in costume and composition. There was much discussion about her moostache, and it changed from white to black, and back to white again. Early in the creative process, she also had a mane of black hair, but that was discarded along the way.

1998

Fiddler on the Hoof

Q: Which billboards have carousels?

A: Clo's Horse, 1988, and Merry Clo Round, 2004

Clodilocks...
and the
three bears

Q: In what other boards does Clo sport a head of hair?

A: **Though Clo always has bangs,** she has a wide variety of colored full heads of hair in Anthony & Cleopatra (1995), Clodilocks (above), Clover the Rainbow (1999), Camelot (2004), Lady Clodiva (2005), Shake, Rattle and Clo (2006), Cowlick (2007), Sumooo Wrestling (2008), No Business Like Clo Business (2008), and Legend Dairy (2009).

* Another interesting "hair" fact is that she has facial hair one time only, with a moostache in Edgar Allan Clo (1998).

Clo's Knit Family

One of Clover's favorites, "Clo's Knit Family" epitomizes the philosophy Clover Stornetta nurtures towards their customers and products.

Clo's Race at Sears Point

Sears Point Raceway (now Infineon Raceway) and Clo join up for the first time to enjoy the need for speed: fast food and fast fun. But Clo knows that *slow food* is the real way to eat.

The oldest cow ever recorded was a Dremon cow named "Big Bertha" that died three months short of her 49th birthday on New Years Eve, 1993.

1999

Our favorite bovine shows her devotion to ecology, as she introduces Clover's line of organic milk.

1999

The New Moollennium

Clo ushered in the new millennium with more dimensional graphics, but kept her perfectly adorable cartoon physique...a cartoon!

Q: How does a cow get to the moon?

A: It flies through udder space!

Clover the Rainbow

We know, the slippers aren't ruby-red, and we weren't allowed to say "Somewhere"!

Q: What other billboard has a famous slipper?

A: Dairy Godmother, 1996

1999

The Sound of Moosic

"Sound of Moosic" was a billboard destined to happen, often-suggested by many fans. We were happy to compose it.

Taken from the "White Cliffs of Dover", "The White Sips of Clover" was posted near the white cliffs of Pt. Arena!
The colors of the cliffs and water were changed three times.

Mooovin' at Sears Point

Sears Point Raceway (now called Infineon Raceway) really got into the spirit of Clo, suggesting both the headline and Clo's spotted car.

2000

Udderly Striking

Clover welcomed 8,000 members of the Women's Bowling League to Sonoma County with this smashing billboard.

Q: What did the bird say when it saw the milk cartons in the grass?

A: Hey! Look at the cow's nest!

This is Clo in her perfect state: sensitive, thoughtful, and naked. We always knew she was an artistic feat, but a cross between Descartes and Rodin?

2000

Wholly Cow

Q: What did the Bull say to the Cow?

A: Will I heifer see you again?

Natural Selection

Q: From the moosical impersonations below, can you identify which billboards they come from?

A: The Sound of Moosic (2000), Shake, Rattle and Clo (2006), Wolfgang Amadeus Moozart (1987), Fiddler on the Hoof (1998)

There have been five remakes in the history of the boards to date:
The Now Cow (1970, page 25, and shown here for 2001), Clo's Line (1976, page 31; 2005, page 132)
Outstanding in Her field (1977, page 32; 2003, page 124; 2009, page 161)
•Splendor in the Glass (1989, page 55; 2005, page 134), and
•Support Your Local Cow (1969, page 23; 2009, page 160).

2001

NASCOW
at Sears Point

CLOVER STORNETTA FARMS

Which billboards feature Clo as a famous artist?

Answers (left to right): Claude Moonet, Micloangelo, Van Clo.

Micloangelo

Fact: Clo loves to imitate her favorite icons. In addition to Micloangelo, Moona Lisa, Clodilocks, Cowpernicus, Van Clo, Clo White, Clopatra, Claude Moonet, Dairy Godmother, Lady Clodiva, Venus de Moolo, Marclo Polo, Clo Magnum, Miss Sonoma Cownty, Wolgang Amadeus Moozart, Christopher Cowlumbus, and Tutankhamoon, Clo is dressing up as her favorite actress, Betty Grable. Can you guess the caption?

2001

Moomaids

Dairy cows can produce
125 lbs of saliva a day.

Dairy Tails

"Dairy Tails" was a headline that was right in line with Clover's puns. This was the first billboard to feature Clo's babies. What a better way to introduce the new herd than with Clo reading her billboard book "Wholly Cow."

2002

Cyclo Therapy

TEAM CLOVER

CLO-TERIUM

Clover sponsored an annual cycling race through the city of Santa Rosa called the Clo-Terium for two years. Proceeds from the Clo-Terium helped benefit non-profits who support the principles of sustainable community and enhance the economic viability, environmental stewardship and social character of Sonoma County. Clover continues the tradition and now sponsors a Clover cycling team, "Team Clo."

Pour It On!

For many years Clover teamed up with Sears Point Raceway, now know as Infineon Raceway, to promote Clover products and promote the track.

Q: Do you remember all the headlines?

A: Clo's Race: 1999,
Mooovin' at Sears Point, 2000
NASCOW, 2001
& Pour It On, 2002

Can you think of some others?

2002

"Marclo Polo" was just the explorer to help people discover the great products of Clover Stornetta Farms. When the agency came up with the headline there were two different visual versions. Some first thought of the great explorer, while others thought of the fun pool game inspired by the explorer's name. The agency, for the first time, and only time thus far, decided to use the same headline with two different images.

Which is your favorite, page 116 or page 117?

2002

Clo's Mooseum

When it came to Clo's Mooseum, we realized we had a herd of masterpieces already.

Q: Can you name the billboards these works of art originated from?

Van Clo

Micloangelo

Moona Lisa

A: Venus De Moolo

Litre of the Pack

Q: Why can't you shock cows?

A: They've herd it all!

Clo's open door policy

FREE FARMED ™

American Humane Association Monitored

Fact: In September, 2000 Clover became the first dairy in the United States awarded the Free Farmed label (now known as American Humane Certified) for humanely produced dairy products. In this billboard Clo holds up the Free Farmed label, proud of Clover's commitment to the welfare of their animals.

Catch Her in the Rye

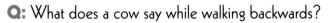

Clover billboards are always a work in process, until they are actually produced. As you can see in these images Clo went from a dancing hula girl to a laid back listener, snapping her finger to the music. We also added two more babies—thus giving the band their name, "The Quartets."

2003

Support Your Local Moooseums!

PACIFIC COAST AIR MUSEUM

CHARLES M. SCHULZ MUSEUM

SONOMA COUNTY MUSEUM

Always conscience of the community, Clover was very proud to support Sonoma County's local museums in this billboard.
Equally proud was the fact that Clo got to make an apprearance with the world famous Peanuts characters.

2003

Outstanding in her field

Originally done in 1977 and shown on page 32, **Outstanding in Her field** has been a signature theme throughout the history of the Clover Stornetta billboard campaign. You can see the latest version done in 2009 on page 161.

Quart of Appeal

Along with the above statue, two other beautifully rendered sculptures of Clo have appeared in the billboard series, first as "Venus de Moolo" (1994), and "Mount Rushmooer" (1997). She is a popular and much sought-after model for artists.

2004

Loclomotion

"Loclomotion" was an idea from Gary Imm, one of the original partners and retired CEO and retired Vice-Chairman of the Board at Clover.

Some people think that cows have four stomachs. Actually, a cow has one stomach with four compartments. Cows are ruminants, which means they regurgitate their food and "chew their cud." The four compartments of their stomach allow them to get the most out of difficult-to-digest foods like grass.

2004

126

Abraclodabra!

Q: What does the invisible man drink for a snack?

A: Evaporated milk!

Camoolot

Q: What was the bull doing in the pasture with his eyes closed?

A: Bull-dozin'!

Merry Clo Round

CLOVER
STORNETTA FARMS

Udderly Silly:

Q: What did the mother cow say to her baby?

A: It's pasture bedtime!

As with previous historical billboards, the agency did quite a bit of research to make sure Lady Clodiva was historically correct. Though Lady Clodiva was quite wealthy in her own right, her husband was taxing her people beyond their ability to thrive, and beyond what she thought was fair. When she complained, her husband challenged her to ride through the streets in the nude if she wanted their taxes reduced. She took that dare, wearing only her long hair for modesty, and her people went inside in respect for her generosity.

By the way, chocolate had nothing to do with it!

2005

In 2005, Clover updated their Organic packaging. "Clo's line" was revised from the 1976 billboard on page 31.
In the new board we added the baby cows using the line as a Volley Ball Net.

2005

The Emporer's New Clo's

It is possible to lead a cow upstairs but not downstairs, because a cow's knees can't bend properly to walk back down.

Splendor in the glass

"Splendor in the glass" first appeared in 1989, on page 55. In 2005 we revised the artwork to include the beautiful vineyards that are so well know in Sonoma, Napa, and Mendocino Counties. In keeping with the setting, Clo sips her milk from a wine glass.

Cloleidoscope

Q: What do you call a group of cattle sent into orbit?

A: The first herd shot round the world!

Everything's coming up Clover

A man's car stalled on a country road one morning. When the man got out to fix it, a cow came along and stopped beside him. "Your trouble is probably in the carburetor," said the cow.

Startled, the man jumped back and ran down the road until he met a farmer. The amazed man told the farmer his story.

"Was it a large red cow with a brown spot over the right eye?" asked the farmer.
"Yes, yes," the man replied.

"Oh! I wouldn't listen to Bessie," said the farmer. "She doesn't know a thing about cars."

2006

Head & tails above the udders

Q: How many different dancing outfits does Clo wear (in the billboards only)?

A: Four: As a ballerina (above, 2006) a can-can dancer (Moolin Rouge, 1996), a choreographer in sweat clothes (ChoreogHEIFER, 1996), and a chorus line girl (Clorus Line, 2006).

Shake, Rattle, & Clo!

In 2006, Clover completely redesigned their Organic packaging. What better way to introduce their new packaging than to have the "King" highlight it in a billboard.

Clorus Line

Twelve or more cows are known as a "flink."
Less than 12 cows are a "kine."

2006

Clo of the Wild

Again, another example of a billboard that started one way, (left with Clo as a jungle she-cow), and finally as Jack London's wonderful Alaskan tale, with the dogs unfortunately having to pull our Clo. But by drinking Clover milk, they were able to do it!

2006

Mooin' in the wind

Clover is the major sponsor of the Clo's Classic football game. Santa Rosa Junior College Bear Cubs host the annual event. All proceeds go to local charities. These charities are picked by the players from the SRJC Bear Cubs. Clo's Classic brings the community together for an afternoon of fun, football and excitement!

2007

Aromootherapy

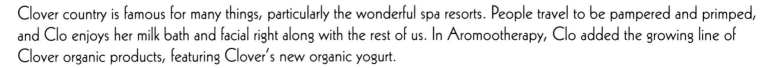

Clover country is famous for many things, particularly the wonderful spa resorts. People travel to be pampered and primped, and Clo enjoys her milk bath and facial right along with the rest of us. In Aromootherapy, Clo added the growing line of Clover organic products, featuring Clover's new organic yogurt.

2007

Cow Lick

The average length of a cow's tongue is 12 inches!

Q: What hair style is a calf's favorite?

A: The cowlick!!!

Q: In what other board does Clo play baseball?

A: None, however on the board "Clo's Call" (page 74), she is the umpire of a baseball game.

Clover Achiever

Q: In what other board does Clo play football?

A: "Scooper Bowl" on page 78).

Q: What did the cow wear to the football game?

A: A jersey!

Amazing Graze

Closephone, Closephone,
Spring cow of Milk, how can we repay
Your contribution to our health?

As you sit sweetly dreaming
Beneath our North Coast sun's rays,
Clover's happy to provide you
With a well-earned Amazing Graze!

Camper: Look at that bunch of cows.
Farmer: Not bunch, herd.
Camper: Heard what?
Farmer: Of cows.
Camper: Sure I've heard of cows!
Farmer: No, I mean a cow herd.
Camper: So what? I have no secrets from cows!

2008

Clover Girl

Q: In what board does the image on the magazine cover appear?

A: "Miss Sonoma County" (page 51).

Q: What did one cow say to the other about the new couple in the dance class?

A: It's like the bovine leading the bovine!

2008

Moo Choice Gracias!

A cow gives nearly 200,000 glasses
of milk in her lifetime.

Three Mooseketeers

As in "Clo of the Wild" and "Something in the Way She Mooves", the first version of "The Three Mooseketeers" was a bit different, minus the King's uniforms in fact.

2008

Clo's dress was modeled after Marilyn Moonroe's dress in the 1954 Twentieth Century Fox movie "There's No Business like Show Business!"

As in past billboards, Deja Mooo went through two ideas before settling on the final version above. Some other Deja jokes:

Deja Moo: The feeling you've drunk this milk before.

Dijon Vu: The feeling you've eaten this mustard before.

Deja Who: The feeling you've heard that Owl before.

Deja Two: The feeling you've had deja vu before.

2008

San FrancisClo

San FrancisClo's poster was signed by Clo and sent to
Mayor Gavin Newsom's office.

Clo's favorite place to go while visiting San Francisclo!

2008

Legend Dairy

Legend Dairy shows past Clo luminaries **Lady Clodiva** (2005), King Clo in **Shake, Rattle & Clo** (2006), **Clopatra** (1995), and the serenely mysterious classic **Moona Lisa** (1990).

(We also considered
Queen Clolizabeth the First,
Clo Washington,
Queen Tut,
& Marilyn Monclo.)

Agricloture

Q: Who is a Cow's favorite Astronomooer?

A: Cowpernicus (Page 92, 1997)

Happily Heifer After

Clo and BeauVine walk into the Sunset, hoof in hoof, happy and content with the beauty of their open pastures, the fresh air, and what the future will bring. Clo knows that the sustainable practices of her farmers keep all her cows in the best of health, and allows Clo to produce milk free of added antibiotics, free of the growth hormone rBST, and quite possibly the cleanest milk in the United States... truly "The milk of Human Kindness." ✍

Q: What other billboards have a Bull?

A: Quartship (2005) & Pitcher Perfect (2007).

2009

Tutankhamoon

Clover joined forces with the de Young Museum and created this billboard to celebrate the exhibition " King Tutankhamun and the Golden Age of the Pharaohs". Also, Clo created coloring pages for the museum, featuring "Tutankhamoon" and "Anthony and Clopatra", which were available for download on the museum web site. The billboard ran on the corner of Lombard and Van Ness Avenues in 2009-2010 .

2009

The Great Clommunicator

Q: What happens when you talk to a cow?

A: It goes in one ear and out the udder!

Support Your Local Cow!

To the side is the first generation of the "Support Your Local Cow" redux!

Outstanding in her field

Outstanding in her field is a favorite of Clo's fans. This remake, in the year 2009, made it the first billboard to have the same headline for a record third time. Can you name the other two years this billboard headline ran?

A: 1977 and 2003

Pitcher of Health

Q: What's black and white and black and white and black and white...?

A: A cow rolling down a hill.

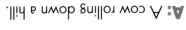

Q: What do you call a cow who works for a gardener?

A: A lawn moo-er.

Q: What do you call cattle with a sense of humor?

A: Laughing stock.

Cowlifornia Dreamin'

In how many billboards does Clo wear glasses?

A: Five:
"Mooin' pitcher star" (1982)
"Clo's Knit Family" (1999)
"Dairy Tails" (2002)
"The Great Clommunicator" (2009)
"Clo ahead, milk my day!" (2009)

2009

Clo ahead, milk my day!

The grand prize winner of Clover Stornetta Farms' 20th Anniversary Billboard Contest, featured above, was Daniel Judd of Rohnert Park, California. He came up with the winning headline, "Clo ahead, milk my day" and won the $5,000 Grand Prize. The billboard contest drew more than 12,000 entries from throughout the United States. Clover and VeVa Communications narrowed the 12,000 entries down to the top twenty. The top three winners out of the twenty were then selected by three prestigious ad agencies: Deutsch, Inc. in Los Angeles, California, The Martin Agency in Richmond, Virginia, and Goody Silverstein and Partners in San Francisco, California.

The second place winning slogan was "You had me at Clo" by Meagan Finnerty of Santa Rosa, California. The third place winner, "Heifer Lasting Love" was submitted by Justin DeFreitas of Berkeley, California.

2009